Who You Would Have Been

SUSANNE JONES KENNEDY

WestBow Press books may be ordered through booksellers or by contacting:

WestBow Press
A Division of Thomas Nelson & Zondervan
1663 Liberty Drive
Bloomington, IN 47403
www.westbowpress.com
844-714-3454

ISBN: 978-1-6642-5816-7 (sc)
ISBN: 978-1-6642-5817-4 (e)

Library of Congress Control Number: 2022903005

Print information available on the last page.

WestBow Press rev. date: 02/28/2022

WESTBOW
P R E S S®
A DIVISION OF THOMAS NELSON
& ZONDERVAN

Dedication

To my precious brother, Mark. We look forward to the day that we can tell you about all the things you have missed.......but until that day we will share your story. Sometimes we will cry, oh but sometimes we will smile when we speak your name.

Every little girl needs a big brother. I was lucky enough to have the very best one! My hero on earth is my angel in heaven. You see, death does not sever the bond between sisters and brothers. Nothing can!

My hope in writing this story is to help the surviving sisters and brothers who are left to pick up the pieces of a shattered world and a broken family, a broken circle.

And to my sweet daddy.......you have now joined Mark in heaven. You waited thirty-two years to see your boy again. As much as we miss you, we can only imagine the reunion the two of you shared. Enjoy your rewards in heaven, Daddy. I'll love you forever, and I will never forget the many lessons you taught me.

This is my story. It is my story of how my family broke.

Many years have come and gone since my brother passed away, but the sting is still fresh. And I am okay with the sting. It reminds me of the love I shared with my brother.

I was blessed to grow up in a pretty much perfect family. Just an all-American family….a daddy, a mama, and three kids. Now, by "perfect" I do not mean we had the best of everything. We had struggles just like any other family. But we did have the best of each other. And at the end of the day, that is what truly matters. Never once did it cross my mind that my world would be torn apart, wrecked, shattered, broken. Oh, but it was. And all of these years later, I am still missing pieces. It is those missing pieces that make me….me. Here is my story of how my family was changed forever.

Oh—how I wonder who you would have been........

—a nurse.....

a lineman.....

a teacher....

——or——

maybe even a preacher!

You stood so tall and strong....

Until one day when something went all wrong!

You had so many goals and dreams to achieve

—Oh, how I wish you didn't have to leave.

You left me too soon.....my heart was so sad.

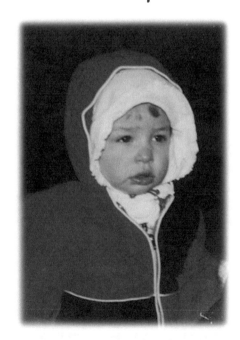

—Sometimes I even find myself mad.

And just who would you be today????
a son.....
a brother.....
a friend......
a husband......
maybe even a dad???????

One thing that I know.....to heaven you did go.

—And I will see you again.....
but until then.....

In my heart you will stay.....
guiding my steps along the way.....
for the love that we shared did not end in death.....
I will love you until my very last breath.

I loved you then, and I love you now!

Our family circle has been broken———
oh———but not for long.

For one day we will see you....that I know for sure.....

Until that day arises....watch over us my brother.

Yesterday, today and tomorrow....

I love you like no other!

**<u>Train up a child in the way he should go, and when he is old
he will not depart from it. (Proverbs 22:6, NIV)</u>**

Growing up, I always remember being happy and feeling loved. Daddy was a preacher. To tell you the truth, Daddy was a Jack of all trades. He would do anything to make money to provide for us. Daddy never thought he was too good to work anywhere. If a floor needed mopping, he'd mop it. If a yard needed cut, he'd cut it. Daddy actually drove a school bus for over 50 years. His selflessness taught me humbleness. Mama taught school for over 20 years. She was able to touch the lives of so many children across the years. Mama was so crafty and creative. You could give her a coffee filter, three rocks and some dirt and she could turn it into the most beautiful Christmas decoration you ever saw. A trait I by no means inherited.

Now, I was pretty lucky in the sibling category as well. I am the baby of the family, and I'm pretty sure that I may have driven my siblings bonkers, but boy did I love them....I still do. You see, love does not end with death. Love does not come untethered when we lose someone that we love. It is simply shown in a different way.

Keep on loving each other as brothers. (Hebrew 13:1, NIV)

In order to really, truly understand my story, you need to get to know who my brother, Mark, was. Marcus Samuel Jones was on born June 9, 1971. He was one of the good ones. He loved Jesus, his family, and football. Mark always had a heart of gold. I have said that it takes most people 100 years to make the same difference in the world that only took Mark eighteen. There was just something different about him. He seemed to always know just where he wanted to go in life. He had a vision. He had a purpose. Mark was destined to do big things. He left for college (Samford University) to play football and study to become a preacher---big plans. But on September 18, 1989 all of those big plans were snuffed out. As Mark was walking off of the practice field, he collapsed…..Mark never got back up. My perfectly healthy football playing brother had died---no warning. He died due to an enlarged heart. How can this happen? Death is a thief…..it stole my brother and robbed him of life.

I still do not understand why he had to die. Why him? I will probably always wonder this, but I will never truly understand the reason why such a great person was taken from my family. It is okay to ask why. It is human nature to need to know…to understand. I have learned this though—even if I knew why my brother had to die—I would still be sad. So, don't lose yourself in the "what-ifs" or the "if only". Cherish the memories. Hold them tight. Write them in a journal so that you can revisit them whenever you want.

One time around 1980 President Carter was running for re-election. His wife, Eleanor Roselynn Carter, was in Alabama campaigning for him. She was in Tuscaloosa to speak at a rally. Well, we all know that for an event of this magnitude, a well-known guest speaker was needed for her introduction. Now in the 1980's in Alabama, there was no bigger name than Paul Bear Bryant. Daddy and Mama took the three of us to Tuscaloosa to hopefully catch a glimpse of The First Lady. As we walked down the road in the direction of the hotel where Mrs. Carter and Bear Bryant would be speaking, Mark stopped dead in his tracks. Putting a hand out and touching daddy, he said with astonishment in his voice, "Daddy, look! That is Bear Bryant." Sure enough, sitting in the passenger seat of his car it was the one and only Coach Paul Bear Bryant. Now, at this time, Mark was about nine years old. With the confidence of a grown man, Mark walked straight up to the Bear, stuck out his hand and said, "Coach, my name is Mark and I am going to play football for you one day." Coach Bryant was so kind with his response. "Son, I don't know if I will still be here when you are old enough to play, but I will tell you this— keep practicing and work hard and you can make it happen." These simple words of encouragement meant the world to Mark. I mean, how many little boys in that day and time could say that THE Bear Bryant had given them advice? Truth is-- I really don't know if Bear Bryant ever realized the impact he had on my brother. He gave Mark hope! I guess you just never know when a small, kind gesture on your part can mean the world to a stranger. Kind words have an impact and can last a lifetime.

September 18, 1989:

The phone rang and my mom answered. For some reason my focus was fixated on her. No matter how hard I try, I will never forget what happened next. I will never forget because that is the exact moment my life was changed forever. It was the moment my family broke. My family broke because the lady on the other end of the line told my mama that my big brother had DIED! I will never forget the look on my mama's face. She dropped the phone and ran outside. Somehow and the tender age of thirteen, I knew I needed to follow her. My sister, Jenny, and I found her collapsed on our neighbor's porch stairs. She was screaming, "He is dead! He is dead!" My dad was at a meeting. This was back in the days before cellphones. We had no way to get in touch with him. A family friend went to the meeting and broke the devastating news to my daddy. I will never forget the moment daddy walked through the door when he finally made it home. He ran straight to my mama. I saw sorrow and brokenness. I saw my world change in the blink of an eye. So begins the "after" part of my life. My story.

Picking Up the Pieces:

In the same way, the Spirit helps us in our weakness. We do not know what we ought to pray for, but the Spirit himself intercedes for us with groans that words cannot express. (Romans 8:26, NIV)

When a child or young person dies –it completely rips apart the family unit. Not only does death steal your loved one, but death robs you of all normalcy. Nothing is the same. Life as you have known it is completely flipped upside down.

No one can prepare you for the hand you have just been dealt. It is an enormous responsibility being the surviving child. It is so overwhelming. You have lost your brother or sister and you are devastated, heartbroken, scared, sick, confused and totally unprepared for your new responsibility……the responsibility of holding your family together….for fixing things…..for being strong when you are at your weakest point……for bending but not breaking.

At the age of thirteen, I had the weight of the world on my shoulders. People are completely unaware of just how stressful it is to be so sad yet feel the necessity to be strong for your parents. It really is a horrible feeling.

I clearly remember people telling me that I needed to be strong for my parents. One of my most vivid memories of this was only a day or so after Mark died. I was so sad. My brother had just died. He was gone forever. I had never known one second of life without my brother and now he was gone. There were so many people in and out of our house in the days that followed his passing. I was trying to hold it all together. Well, I broke! I started to cry (totally natural). Big, fat, REAL tears were streaming down my face. My heart felt like it was literally broken. A lady that I had known most of my life walked up to me and pointed her finger in my face and said, "You better not let your parents see you crying!" Now, I am sure she meant well, but boy did those words cut me like a knife. It added an immeasurable amount of pressure to the already terrible situation. I vividly remember trying to stop crying, but I just couldn't. I went to my bedroom and crawled in my closet, shut the door and cried….and cried….and cried. After a while I could hear my mom calling for me. I didn't answer her calls…because after all, "I better not let her see me cry!" Finally, I collected myself as much as possible and opened the door. The same lady who had scolded me earlier walked in my room as I climbed out of my closet. She gave me the coldest look and told me that I had upset my mama because I hadn't answered her when she called for me. At that point, it felt like everything I did was wrong. What was I supposed to do? Act like everything was just fine and dandy?? No child…no person… should ever have that amount of pressure on him/her. Like I said, I am sure this lady's intentions were good—but her words and her actions that day forever impacted me. Mostly because I believed her. I believed that I better not let my parents see me cry. The truth is—it is perfectly okay to grieve in front of your parents. You CAN let them see you cry.

Truthfully, you must grieve too. Healing is necessary and so are tears. Tears nor time will heal your heart completely, but believe it or not….you will smile again. Believe it or not, you will be able to talk about your brother, sister or loved one and you will laugh again. You will find your smile again, and you will keep moving forward. Day by day….step by step!

Never compare your grief to someone else's. You should never feel guilty for being sad or for grieving. Just because someone else is suffering from a "bigger" or "fresher" loss, does not mean you do not have the right to be sad too. Cry all you want! It is your new way to express your love for your lost loved one. Love does not end when a person dies. It is simply revealed differently.

We don't know the day or the time that we will die. Honestly, we most likely do not even want to know. But unfortunately, we are now well aware of just how fleeting life is. I can tell you this, none of this is your fault. You should never toil with the idea that maybe it should have been you and not your sibling. I have to admit that I did that. My mama and daddy had one boy and two girls. If I had died…..if it had been me and not Mark, at least they one have one of each, a boy and a girl. Never let yourself think this way!

Mike Wixon wrote for the Mississippi Press in 1989. His words in his article printed after Mark passed away were so true then and they still ring true today.

"Just like the football game ends when the clock runs out and the final horn sounds, our lives end when our time is up. Unlike football, however, we don't know the timetable on our lives. We cannot see the clock ticking behind the end zone." (Mike Wixon, MS Press).

Because he lived, they learned.

Although none of Mark's nieces and nephews had the chance to meet him, the life he lived impacted each of them in ways that maybe only they can explain. Each one has been influenced by his death, but more importantly, they have been impacted by his life. And it is the life that he lived that I hope to honor with this book. Mark shouldn't be remembered because he died; he should be remembered because he lived! And he lived fully and passionately!

When I imagine what my family would look like if Uncle Mark was still with us, there is no doubt that life would be much different. There would be more belly-aching laughter, more harmless pranks pulled, and, I'm sure, many more stories told. I would have a strong shoulder to cry on when things in life feel just a little too hard to handle. One thing that my Uncle Mark has been teaching me my entire life is that tomorrow isn't promised. I recently lost my Granddaddy. I now realize that it is when we lose a person we love so deeply, we must learn to embrace the memories and continue to create moments full of joy and pure happiness. The difference now is that all of those happy times will also be combined with heartache because we no longer have that person with us to experience those wonderful moments with......and that is okay.

It is hard to put into words all that I have learned from a man I never got the opportunity to meet. It's difficult to compile all of the questions I have for him. It's more of a feeling. A feeling of knowing that my Uncle Mark knows me, sees me, and is with me every day. --Samantha

It is unbelievable to think how much you can learn from somebody that you have never met. I have heard so many stories about my uncle and the man that he was. He was a man of God! He has shown me to never take life for granted! You're never guaranteed anything in life, so you should never leave anything on the table! It truly is an honor to be his namesake. My Grandaddy was so proud of him! You could always look at Grandaddy's smile and know how much he loved him! —Mark

Thinking about what life would be like today if my Uncle Mark were here makes me wonder about all the endless memories that could have been made. It is unreal how someone I never met could leave an impact on me. Hearing stories about his hard work and determination through his football career and relationship with the Lord is inspiring. Although he was only on this Earth for eighteen very short years, Uncle Mark left an impact that would last in his family for generations to come. With the thought of my mother losing a brother, a very best friend, this makes me cherish every single moment that I am with my brother and family. I am grateful for the uncle I never knew. —Karlie

I don't know you. I don't know what you sound like. I don't know what you really look like. I've only heard stories, but I know I love you, and you are going to love me too. --- McKenzie Brooke

Growing up without Uncle Mark put a ginormous question mark in my life. I heard all of these stories about him and each story made me want to make something of my life. At the same time it made me cherish life, and it gave me the realization of how short it is. I really wish I could have at least met my uncle, and I wish that I knew why God took him from us. One day I may figure that out, but until then I will keep trying to grow closer to God and will seek to be as strong as my Grandad." --Jacob

A sweet message from Jenny, my sister, to Mark:

No one could replace you. Everyone who knew you loved you. Handsome, strong, unique, willing, and clever describe you. My childhood friend, my brother. I treasure the many good times and memories, but I wanted more. So, until we meet again - I love you forever! --Jenny

True friendship is a rare treasure and often hard to find. Mark was blessed in his short life to have many amazing friends. Below are some special memories shared by some of his dearest friends.

My memories of Mark are that of a kind spirit with a connection to the Lord beyond his years. He remains in my mind as one of the most devout Christians I have ever known. However, he was a real person that never avoided talking about his weaknesses though they were few. To this day, I have thoughts of what or how would Mark handle situations that I deal with daily in my life. That speaks to the powerful impression he left on my life and those that knew him well.

My favorite story about Mark involves football during our 9th grade year. About his time, he discovered that this would be his sport, and he put everything into being the best player he could be. On one particular day, I was matched up against Mark at practice. Mark, being a great friend, he really did not come at me hard and I was on the spot at the next game. Believe me, that would never happen again. I can truly say that I think that week helped Mark realize what he had to do to be the great player that he became for the rest of his football life. He loved the game and overachieved beyond imagination through hard work. So proud that he had the chance to go to Samford University.

I most remember that Mark was a friend to all people and had a really big heart for anyone disadvantaged in the world. As much sorrow as we all felt losing him, I cannot help but think the Lord said, "Good job son. I am taking you home!" –Eddie Anderson

I first met Mark our 10th grade year at spring training. As the young group of offensive linemen, we became a close group and remain that way to this day. Mark was an impressive athlete that was as strong as he needed to be, but it was not in his nature to make anyone look bad……which he was capable of doing at will.

We had some great times playing ball, but that is not where my love for Mark comes from. He was the kindest, most caring person I have ever known. He could lead a person to do the right thing by his actions alone. He didn't have to tell you how strong his faith in the Lord was, you could see it in the way he carried himself.

Mark helped shape me into the person I am today. I guess it's not meant for me to understand why he was taken so soon but I love him and miss him. ---Mark Wade

In 1989 Mark attended Samford University in Birmingham, Alabama. These are some of his journal entries that he wrote in his short time as a student there. My purpose in including these is to allow you to gain insight to the things that Mark found most important in life. I have included them just as he wrote them…..mistakes and all. Remember, these journals were typed on a typewriter long before computers and autocorrect were available. Look beyond the typos and misspelled words and focus on the message……..a message that all of these years later still teaches others about what is most important in life. Many valuable life lessons can be learned from the most imperfect things. These journal entries are not grammatically perfect, but the lessons found in each one are flawless and timeless.

Mark Jones
Journal Entry 1

My relationlhip with the Lord is the most important thing In my life. When I was growing up I was always exposed to church and taught to live my life as God would have me to live it. However, the topic that kl would like to talk about now is not just church or my knowledge of God 's work, but my personal relationship to God. This personal relationship that I have with the Lord drives me in my everyday life, it inspires me to be the best that I can be, and It is what kl try to base all of my words and deeds on.

I was a tery young boy when I was baptized. This baptist, although important was ndt the experience that I thought that It should be. For years thereafter I felt something missing from my life. This missing part was something that I could never really explain. The subj ect of this missing part was a subj ect that I could never really confront with comfort. My life was one of good deeds but one with a big question mark in front of it. A question mark not to be answered until years later.

Real salvation was a question that, although I would talk about it, I would never examine myself to see If I had this salvation. When I was sixteen years old I finally got the nerve to opem up and ask myself the most important question that any person can ask themselves. That Is the question, "Am I really saved?" When I could not honestly give a positive answer I knew that there were changes to be made In my 11fe•.So right then and there I asked the Lord to save me.

Every since that night that I erased all of my doubts of my salvation my life has not been the same. Now my life is one in wich I not only live a good life, but it is a life that Is filled with assurance and the knowledge that I have a home in heaven. My witnessed has become much greater because of the confidence that God has given me and the assurance that I now know that I have because of the gifts of God. I now live a life that is filled with joy because of the gifts that God has given me. I would like to challenge anyone who reads this journal to open up their hearts and see if they have something missing in tetr lives and I would like to tell them that something is probably God.

Mark Jones
Journal Entry 2

My friends meen a great deal to me. I have many friends with whöm I am. close toand my life would not be the same without them. My friends are not a specific type of people, they are just very close to me. My friends are not people whom I have really selected out of a crowd they are just those who are my friends because they choose to be. My friends can lift me up when I 'm feeling down. There been many situations in my Ilfe that my friends have helped me fight through. Every time I feel alone or am hurting just talking to friends can gtve me the encouragement that it takes to make it thoughthese hard times.

My best friends are my friends out of choice they arenot close to me because of anything I can give them or anything I can offer. This friendship by choiceis what makes my friends so special to me. The fact that they love me for who I am and not for what I can give them is very heartwarming.

My friends have a variety of charicteristicsand are not just as a mold, One of my best friends is a Vietnamese immigrant. These people are not people that I sit back and choose from the crowd they are peoplewho I have gotten close to from football. They are claSsmates and fellosq church members. My friends come from a variety of different places and they are a variety of different kinds of people.

My life would be very different and very strange without the pedple whom I call my friends. My friends give me hope. They give me a person to talk to when I j really need one. My friends are a special breed of people because I can see see the way that they redlly are and that Is what makes friendship so special.

24

Mark Jones
Journal Entry 3

My mother Is one of the dearest persons In my 11 fee My mother
is probably the most loving and caring person In my life. She is
a very Christian woman and she has very high Christian morals
and pr!nciples. From my earliest childhood she has taken great
care of me and she has always put the wants and needs of of
the rest of my family ahead of the wants and needs of herself.
Myk mom is wowan willing to sacrifice for the needs of others.
She is a wowan willing tofight for rights and principles that
she holds so very true in her life.

My mother wasa raised ᵃ in the same town that I was raised in.
She is like me in many different ways. We both hold God at the
highest place in our life. We both are very family oriented and
we care a great deal about the other people in our family. Our
closeness now is being strengthened by my life as a college
student. Now that I am away from my mother our relationship has
been strengthened by our *absence from one another, College
life has taght me how much my mother really means to me.

I am now going through what my mom has spent my whole life
preparing me for. Now that I am on my own I am more independen
and I have to rely, more own myself and my own abilities and
not the abilities of my mom. I don't beleive that I would be
able to make it on my own if It weren't for my morn' s help.

The lessons learned from my mom arelessons that will last a
lifetime. The memories of the good times that I 've had withmy
mom areones that can't be replaced. So tomy mother I give
thanks for al lof these wonderful things.

Mark Jones
Journal Entry 4

The person that I most admire in my life is my father. He has alvVays been there for me when I needed someone to talk to. My father has always put the welfare of me and the rest of my familyahead of the wnts and needs of himself. My father not only is a good man, he is a good christian man. He puts Cod at the center of his life and trusts him with all of his heart. My dad has always been there for me and I know that even now when I am away at college he is with me in spirit even though he cannot be with me in body.

It ^{I}s hard fbr me now. I feel alone being away from my father as well as the rest of my family, All of my life we have been together and for the first time ever I 'm on my own. I always knew that It would be hard when I left home but I never had experienced it. Every night I lay awake in bed dreaming of me and my dad getting together over the Christmas holidays and going on a nice little camping trip or just sitting around and talking together about old timesand getting reaquainted.

I beleive that you never really know how much you love someone until you are away from them. My feelings for my dad and my love for him have grown stronger every day that I 'm away from him. My mind is filled with joy and longing when I hear from my father on the !phone. It brings a good feeling to my heart just to talk to him on the phone and here him tell me of all of the goings on back home. Thinking about getting together with my father once again helps me to make through all of the schoolwork and the football practices we have.

Well I guess that it's time for me to grow up and become a man myself. Although my dad Is not here for all of the time his lessons about life and all of the things that he has taught me are. I owe a great deal to my dad. My father has taught me a great deal about life. And just Knowing that he's still there for me when I get back gives me a warm feeling inside.

Mark Jones
Journal Entry 5

Football is one of the most enjoyable and interesting activities In my life. To me football provides recreation and It gives me a challenge and a sense of meaning In my life. I started playing football In the eighth grade and I never dreamed that I would play college football, but that distant dream has become a reality .

Here I am today a college football player and facing one of the toughest moments in my 11 fee I have been playing college ball now for about five weeks and I 'm at the bottom if the barrel again. Football Is a challenge in much the same way that life Is a challenge. Being on the bottom helps me to dream greater dreams and have more determination than many of my teammates. The challenge of being on the bottom will also make success much sweeter,

The wait to play will be long but familiar, I had to wait until my last year in both high school and In jr high to ever really play. This is why the wait to play in college will not be as bad to me as it will to many of my teammates, This wait will make it seem much sweeter when I finally do play.

Football adds a great deal to my schedule, In my first week and! a half it has alréady caused me to slip behind greatly. guess all that I can do is buckle down and take the extra load. The benefits of football are too great to quit because, of a heavy load,

So I ¹ ll just take it as it comes and play the game,

Mark Jones
Journal Entry 6

Family. This is a topic that weighs haevl.ly on my mindat this time. Family. This Is one of the most vluable things In my life. I have really been reminded of that fact over the last couple of weeks. I have been away from my family for five or six weeks now and except for two weekend v Islts I have been away from my family for the first time In my 11 fee

The excitement of a new Ilfe away from home is one of the greatest and most challenging things in my life. As exciting as this Is it is not as exciting as the thought of seeing my family on the holidays. My family and I are extremely closeand this closeness, despite what one might think, is strengthenedby our seperation.

Being away from my family has brought me closer to them, I guess that you never know how much something means to you until you have to part with it. This weekend I plan to go to a family reunionand for a short period of time become reaquainted with some moe distant relatives. My immediate family won't be able to make it due to the health of my grandmother. So being with with relatives, even outside of my immediate familywill be heartwarming.

Family Is somethiong that can't be replaced, I long for the day that I can be with my family again. I can't wait until I that feeling comes back that only family can bring, Until next Monday I'll be with family so you can expect an Interesting Journal on Monday.

MARK JONES

ENGLISH 103.03
9- 15 -89

Home

    Home is like no other place in the world. jjMy home cannot be replaced by any other. Home is a special place to me and it is a place that has made my life what it is today. My home is filled with great memories of people whom I am close to. Home to me is a special place that is filled with friends and family that hold a very special place in my heart.

    Home is not just a place for me it is a spirit. The spirit of home is a feeling that I feel very strongly in my life right now. My new life as a college student has given me the experience of being away frotn home and being off on my own for the first time in my life. This new life has strengthened my feelings for horne rnore than anyth i ng I have experienced before.

Bible Verses for Comfort:

He will wipe away every tear from their eyes. There will be no more death or mourning or crying or pain, for the old order of things has passed away. (Revelation 21:4, NIV)

Blessed are those who mourn, for they will be comforted. (Matthew 5:4, NIV)

The Lord is close to the brokenhearted and saves those who are crushed in spirit. (Psalms 34:18, NIV)

Come to me, all you who are weary and burdened, and I will give you rest. (Matthew 11:28, NIV)

*I truly pray that in some small way this book helps
you on your journey through grief.*

The Holy Bible: New International Version. Grand Rapids: Zondervan, 1984.

Special memories from friends and loved ones:

_____
_____
_____
_____
_____
_____
_____
_____
_____
_____
_____
_____
_____
_____
_____
_____
_____
_____
_____
_____
_____
_____
_____
_____
_____
_____
_____
_____
_____

Some of my most favorite memories:

Printed in the United States
by Baker & Taylor Publisher Services